awake

be the witness of your thoughts

the elephant hauls himself from the mud

in the same way drag yourself

out of your sloth

buddha

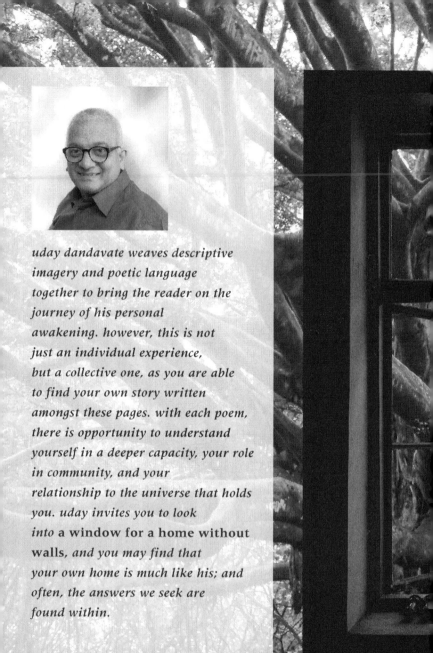

uday dandavate weaves descriptive
imagery and poetic language
together to bring the reader on the
journey of his personal
awakening. however, this is not
just an individual experience,
but a collective one, as you are able
to find your own story written
amongst these pages. with each poem,
there is opportunity to understand
yourself in a deeper capacity, your role
in community, and your
relationship to the universe that holds
you. uday invites you to look
into a window for a home without
walls, and you may find that
your own home is much like his; and
often, the answers we seek are
found within.

a window for a home without walls

life
imagination
design

poems by
uday dandavate

a window
for a home
without
walls

life
imagination
design

poems by
uday dandavate

a window for a home without walls
poems on life imagination & design

author:
uday dandavate

editor:
molly pearson

design:
mookesh patel

this book is the result of an inspired
isolation during covid-19 isolation
and lockdown.

the book is published by the author.
© 2020, uday dandavate,
san francisco, california.

isbn 9798645956455

printed by kindle direct publishing

software:

adobe illustrator
adobe indesign
adobe photoshop

typeface:
meridien
bold • bold italics
7 • 9.5 • 14 • 20

tracking:
25 • 30
leading:
7/12 • 9.5/15 • 14/29 • 20/29

it all began with casual linkedin chat on 23 april 2020
during the coronavirus lockdown. uday shared
some designs for his book and the poems intrigued me
much more.

reading his poems is an experience — like strolling
in a forest. away from the engagements of a city
and immersed in the melody and tranquility of nature.
a space wherein to reflect, rediscover and explore
appropriate avenues in life, imagination and design.

*in a **designerly way** my mind connects the swiss designer*
adrian frutiger's meridien typeface with his poems.
sixteenth century typeface inspired frutiger to create an
alphabet without any straight strokes, and he
hoped the reader of a text set in this typeface would feel
as though wandering through a forest. meridien is
at once sharp, graceful, arresting, and sensuous; much
like a forest — like uday's poems.

thus, evolved the design of this book. the titles remain
in the same location — like the north star — the navigator.
the images represent my personal and emotional
interpretations of individual poems, just as readers
continue to develop their own perspectives,
reflections and actions.

enjoy.

mookesh patel

contents

to my mother

who taught me

not to fear

&

to my father

who taught me

to always

be an optimist

" these poems have a voice that

speaks to humanity in

people who are crying out for

freedom and hope.

poems, like music, have a

healing effect. at a time when

humanity is violating

foundational principles of

nature, these poems

invite the reader to join

in the process of

healing and restoration.

we all have buddha's

restlessness, curiosity and

enlightenment in us,

but we don't feel it because

we do not allow life to

enter our consciousness.

as we become more

aware we gain the capacity to

participate in the process

of evolution and creation. we

must participate in this

process anonymously, with

consciously cultivated

subtlety and moderation."

prof. mohan bhandari

a visionary co-creator of

design foundation program

at national institute of design

an unstuck feather

a gentle breeze

lifted the feather

and carried it away

as i reached out to catch it.

i was disappointed that my craving

for the soft and tender feel

of the feather

my desire to own it

was not fulfilled yet

as the feather disappeared

and blended with the landscape

and the cold breeze

brought me goosebumps

i had a moment of clarity:

i am the feather.

i was meant to belong

to a mother bird

i had a distinct identity

that was tied to my flock

i was meant to be

one amongst many

15

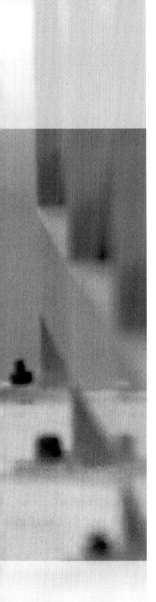

not meant to drift away.

it was imprinted in me

that just like humans

feathers are social.

but my circumstances

and my loose connection

to my flock

got me unstuck.

i feel closer to nature

i feel free to wander

free from the weight of my ego

fear does not stop me

i love riding the winds

my weightlessness

and my wings

allow me to

twist and turn

and dive and dance and

take a leap towards

abundant possibilities

do not try catching me

do not try holding on to me

do not try putting me back

the true joy

is in letting me fly

in letting me brush by you

bringing you stories

bringing you love

creating tenderness.

you may think that   *strangers are friends*

i do not have a purpose   *wilderness is home*

that i am a drifter   *ambiguity is peaceful*

but that's not true: *unpredictability my intrigue and*

like the waves of the ocean   *chaos my strength*

and the passing clouds   *i am who i am*

and the changing colors of the sky   *because i am*

inspiring in you   *an unstuck feather*

curiosity for possibilities and

openness to chance encounters.

inspiring your imagination

i woke up today

with a realization

that today is

the day of celebration

of rising from the dead

to spread love and

compassion

i am an atheist

yet i believe

there is a god inside us

who we crucify every day.

with greed

and impatience

with speed

and impertinence.

temples do not

give us relief

from the burden

of our guilt

prayers do not

give us freedom

from the haunting

voice of our conscience

holy books do not

bring us awakening

that we lost when

we lost compassion

closing our eyes

to meditate does not

open our hearts to

the sufferings of others

congregations

do not bring us strength

that we lose

by creating divisions

there is a god inside us

who we crucify every day

today

we cannot go to our temple

we cannot seek atonement

we cannot congregate

we cannot indulge our desires

but today

from the confines

of our conscience

we have an opportunity

to atone for our acts

of violence

against nature

and humanity.

today

we have an opportunity

to resurrect the god

inside us

23

*a window for a home
without walls*

before designing

a window

i search for direction.

i break the walls

that surround me

i clear my view

let my mind wander

searching for the direction that

will

guide my curiosity

and give me inspiration.

before designing

a window

i search for focus.

i imagine

a home without walls

and search for

a point of focus

for letting my mind

rest in stillness

i let my surroundings

enter my consciousness

stimulate my senses and

bring me calmness and clarity

before designing a window

i find my purpose:

do i want to

feel spiritual and

be left alone or

engage with the world?

do i want to invite

nature into my home?

do i want to

have conversations with a bird?

do i want to

smell the grass and

feel the breeze

or just lay there

my imagination

keeping aloof from

the sensations of the world?

i design a window

in my imagination

as i stand in a home

without walls

designing journeys

back then

i believed that

like making a movie

a journey could be designed

i believed

a journey must have a plot

a script and a storyboard

that it should have locations

characters and costumes

i believed that

just like a movie

a well designed journey

could evoke

preprogrammed emotions.

it must incorporate

a climax

i believed that

a journey design

must include

delightful touchpoints

and a happy end

i believed i could write

a script and a storyboard

for an ideal journey

for others to take.

understanding comics

helped me

understand

journeys are more like comics

than like movies.

journeys are

creations of the imagination

designing journeys

is like designing comics.

a more restrained illustration

leaves more

for people to fill in

with their imagination

and make it their own

a well designed journey

is self created.

emotions are authentic

the plot is organic

in an ideal journey

the end does not matter

the purpose

the experience

the meaning

rise to the top

no matter what the end

a well designed journey

mirrors a well lived life:

it has a purpose

it has compassion

it has values

it has ethics

it has courage

it has hope

it has strength

it has love

it has pain

it has resilience

it has poetry

above all

a well designed journey

creates memories.

the end of an ideal journey

is like the end of a well lived life.

in the words of leonardo da vinci

a well spent day

brings happy sleep

so a life well used

brings a happy death

creativity

creativity is not

expertise

it is an innate capacity.

just as

each of us has emotions

we also have creativity in us

just as an emotion is

an impulse to act

creativity is an impulse

to act with purpose

to express

to solve a problem

to overcome a barrier

to resolve a deadlock

creativity reframes our perception

of problems

as opportunities to find solutions

of dead ends

as an invitation to find new paths

of darkness

as an incentive to light a candle

of anger within us

as an impetus to fight injustice

yes you can

harness your innate creativity

by believing in it and

by practicing it

by knowing that

when we run out of options

there is yet another way

waiting to be found.

when we are at a loss for words

there is yet another way

of expressing

when we hit a roadblock

there is yet another path

waiting to be discovered

when we are faced with a problem

there is a solution

waiting to be found

when we are at a loss of words

there is yet another way

of expressing yourself

nature gave us the creative capacity

so we can keep living purposefully

try using it.

nature gave us the creative capacity

so we can keep living purposefully

perspectives

i often wonder why

people let hatred build up.

simmering hatred

hurts the hater more

than the hated.

i wonder maybe

hate is tied to

paucity of

self esteem

self confidence and

self making.

when we are comfortable

in our own skin

our view of others

stems from

a more secure place

than when our self esteem

is vulnerable to

doubt

criticism

adversity or

disagreement

i often wonder

if only

people were driven

more by love

than by hatred

wouldn't the world be

a better place?

so how might we

help people

hate less and love more?

we must not

retaliate

punish or

condemn those

who are consumed

with hatred

instead we must

find ways to

heal them

nourish them

and cultivate in them

hope

confidence

resilience and

a creative outlet
.

instead we must

help them understand

that everything disagreeable

is so because

people have different perspectives

and that

a different perspective

is not a conspiracy

against their perspective

nor an attack on

their beliefs

that it is

the nature of the universe

to have

multiple perspectives

multiple beliefs

multiple goals

multiple pathways and

multiple journeys

while compatible perspectives

may lead to

harmonious outcomes

diverse perspectives

evoke curiosity

encourage critical thinking

inspire creativity and

lead to innovation

hatred is the escape

of the meek.

hatred impairs imagination.

to overcome hatred

we must overcome fear

overcoming fear

opens the door for

more options

more exposure

more learning

more growth and

enhanced potential

let us therefore

conquer hatred and

open our minds

to explore

infinite possibilities

dear ceo

how confident are you of

your future?

do you know when

covid 19 will clear

consumer spending will resume

supply chains will resume

your stock will rise and

your employees will return

to a purposeful career?

how reliable is your data

in projecting the future?

you are not alone.

nobody knows

when covid 19 will pass

when the rising curve of death

will bend towards the bottom

if the hands without work and

stomachs without food

will rise in outrage

when nothing is clear

one thing is clear:

that nature is healing

families are bonding and

new communities are forming

while people are trapped

in their homes

they are wandering inside

listening to the voice

of their conscience

questioning their past

and waiting for a new future

to emerge from the ashes

the future is emerging

from the restlessness

of the mind

from the devastation

of the economy

from the crashing

of hopes

from the pangs

of hunger

and the cravings

of the heart

you can reimagine a new future

not from your factories

not from your reserves

but from the shared values

shared dreams

and shared culture

people retain

imagine this:

you have lost everything

if i were you

your assets

i would disregard data

your market

reject wall street

but you still have

stop listening to

your people

the politicians

their shared purpose

and tune myself to

their wisdom

the reverberations of

their values

searching souls

their competencies and

their imagination.

what would you build?

design is

design is not an artifact

design is an act

of imagining possibilities

and bringing them to life

design neither begins

nor ends with designers

it begins in the social imagination

and lives where it is meant to

in people's routines

rituals and habits

good design invites people

to make it their own

good design

stimulates imagination

and invites creativity

good designers are

humble

empathic

and supportive

of people's craving

for meaning making

good designers

build scaffolds

for imagining and experiencing

life on our own terms

how to be a mindful
ethnographer

be present

look

don't search.

be alert

be aware

don't focus.

be patient

empathize

don't judge.

be curious

understand

but don't summarize.

participate

but don't get involved.

empty your mind

collect the data

but don't connect the dots yet.

scribble notes

doodle diagrams

put away your laptop

ask questions

probe deeper

don't argue.

encourage them to

show and tell

and to express their opinions

but hold back yours.

be sincere

be courteous

don't get emotional.

show interest

in their culture

in their etiquette

but don't bring up politics

or religion.

respect their silence

interpret it

don't interrupt it

respect their energy

reinforce it

don't be an imposition.

respect their time

use it prudently

but don't overstay your welcome

be friendly to them

to their family and pets

because you may have to

go back for more insights

you will be surprised

being rational

with those feeling emotional

being sensitive

to those who are insensitive

giving love

to those feeling hateful

you will be surprised with the results.

asking for help

from those who are helpless

asking for charity

from those who are poor

speaking in a soft voice

to a noisy audience

being kind

to those who are angry at you

asking questions

to those who don't want to listen to you

caring for those

who don't care

paying attention when

nothing seems to be happening

listening to sounds

in a quiet place

giving away something

you want to hold on to

reaching out

to people you don't know

asking advice

from people you think don't know much

seeking strength

from people who are weak

listening

to those who have given up talking to you

listening

to those who don't have a voice

transcending biases

and opening our minds

has its rewards.

you will be surprised

that there is more to it

than meets the eye

energy fields

have you noticed?

when we are smiling

positive energy fields surround us

in which others feel positive

when we feel upset

tense energy fields surround us

in which others feel tense

when we feel livid

unwelcome energy fields surround us

in which others feel unwelcome

when we feel insecure

uncertain energy fields surround us

in which others feel vulnerable

we could create a positive energy field

only if we could control our feelings but...

feelings are hard to control

because they are tied

to our interpretations

it is hard to challenge

our interpretations

because they are tied

to our beliefs

it is hard to challenge

our beliefs

because they are tied

to our self image

it is hard to challenge

our self image

because it is tied

to our ego

if we can't control our feelings

how do we cultivate

a positive and playful energy field?

how do we sustain

a welcoming and nurturing space?

people are drawn

not as much to our words

not as much to our personality

not as much to our adornments

but to our energy field

they call it our aura

i have learned

that a sense of detachment

from our ego

a break from needless interpretation of everything

helps overcome

intentions and expectations

a compassionate soul

a caring glance

a gentle touch

a soft breath

a slow pace

in a quiet environment

creates an energy field

in which friendships grow

trust is nurtured

confidence is built

productivity is enhanced

and love prevails

we are only

a forest

means more than

a count of

the trees in it

wilderness

means more than

a land untouched

by human habitation

ecology

means more than

a collection of life forms

that support

each other within it

being human

means more than

being kind compassionate

and responsible

progress

means more than

the lands we conquer

the skies we cover

the rivers we harness

the distances we reach

the mysteries we resolve

the homes we build

the machines we invent

and the species we kill

for the sake of development

those who fail to respect

the principles of the universe

the design of nature

the rules of coexistence

those who fail to understand

that in the vastness

of the universe

we are only

a microorganism

in the abundance of nature's design

human progress

only creates imbalance

nature's creation is a common ground

the skies the oceans

the rivers the mountains

the forests the birds

the insects the animals

the flora and fauna

creates in us

a shared sense of purpose:

to live and let live.

the colors of the skies

the gentle touch of the breeze

the sounds of the crickets

the sight of approaching rain

57

the smell of wet earth and

the taste of ocean waters

create in us

a sense of invitation

to be inspired and creative.

in the process of evolution

human ambition

only serves as an aberration

we must remember

the words of

the wise man einstein

when the bees become extinct

the humans

will not be far behind

a search for purpose

when we are surrounded

by the skies and the ocean

by the stars and the glow worms

by the trees that rise to the sky

and the grass below

by the pitch darkness of the night

by the sound of water

falling from the skies and gushing through the river

by the rainbow

that begins in one land and disappears to the other

we feel a sense of

unity in diversity.

when we witness

the clouds pass by   *they create a realization*

the birds fly by   *that the only thing permanent*

the animals migrate   *is change*

the seasons change

                                          when we see a sunset

                                          a withering flower

                                          a wild animal dragging its prey

a dead fly on the windowpane

a baby bird

that has fallen from its nest

we experience

inevitability

vulnerability

it creates in us

a search for purpose

nature gives to us

the reason

to pursue a shared purpose

and create a common ground.

let us tap into our memories

while keeping our dreams alive

let us tap into our wisdom

while keeping our curiosity intact

life is short

let us give it a shot

just to be

as i stumbled

and rebalanced

i noticed the rock

i had tripped over.

as pain shot through my body

it faced me nonchalantly

as if to say

how clumsy of you!

i've been sitting here for ages.

i've survived

thunderstorms tornados

wildfires tsunamis

earthquakes and hurricanes.

nothing deters me.

my purpose is just

to be.

people step on me

to rise up

they sit on me

when they are tired

they trip over me

when they are careless

they stare at me

when they are clueless

they paint on me

when they feel creative

they write their names on me

when they want to be

a part of history

birds perch on me

so they can sing

fish slide under me

so they can be safe

and i sit here undeterred

because i am a rock.

my purpose is just

to be

i don't get swayed

by emotions

you may scratch my back

but i won't scratch yours

i don't have an agenda

i don't throw my weight around

i know you have a life

and you must keep going.

i don't need your attention.

when you get emotional

i remain stoic

you have needs but

i am not needy.

my purpose is just

to be

i am a rock.

i will be here

just in case

our paths cross again

my purpose is just

to be

what if

giving

without expectations

creates motivation

to pay it forward

loving

without expectations

nourishes the soul

touching

without expectations

cultivates intimacy

caring

without expectations

builds empathy

painting

without intentions

cultivates spontaneity

dancing

without intentions

releases inhibitions

wandering

without intentions

uncovers the unexpected

observing

without intentions

or expectations

enhances awareness

conversing

without intentions

or expectations

builds understanding

listening

without intentions

or expectations

overcomes biases

it is true:

intentions can bring us closer to our goals

and

expectations can satisfy our emotions

but what if freeing ourselves from

intentions and expectations

could free us from

doubt disappointment distrust

apathy & anger

bias or boredom

mental blockages

tunnel vision

and even

stagnation

in the absence of intentions

and expectations

we rediscover ourselves

strange are
human aspirations

we reach out · *we aspire to become*

to the unreachable · *someone we are not*

but evade the embrace · *while discarding*

of what we have · *who we truly are*

we delve in to dreams · *we seek to solve*

but neglect · *the mysteries of the world*

the present · *but fail to discover*

at hand · *the world inside ourselves*

we seek those · *we seek answers from others*

who don't care · *but overlook our own unsolved questions*

while abandoning

those who never left us · *we seek justice*

but we neglect others' needs for fairness.

we run to catch up · *we pine for freedom*

but bypass · *but dismiss responsibilities*

where we stand

we seek to

cross the horizon

but fail to

define boundaries

we want to be heard

but we don't care to listen

strange are human aspirations

we neglect to look at ourselves

the past, the current & the future

as i ponder the end of one year

and the beginning of another

i wonder

what holds more

meaning to me:

the past

the present or

the future?

then i think about the river

sitting by the river

i always compare

life with river.

a life filled with

purposeful experiences

feels like the

journey of a river

a river is a river.

it's a home to marine life within

it shapes landscapes

along its banks

and gives birth to

civilizations over time.

stagnant waters

do not make a river

nor do stagnant minds

make a living being.

a river must

keep flowing.

a river must

nurture life and

be large hearted

and stomach

the good the bad

and the ugly.

so what does

the passing of the old

and arrival of the new year

mean to me?

i long to be a river.

i want to spread

love compassion and creativity

to nurture kindness

to help evolve a new civilization

that is empathic cooperative

and trusting.

i want to irrigate minds

so positivity hope and

optimism will grow.

i do believe

no matter how dry

the terrain in the inner world

that sprinkling compassion

will bring back the spring of life.

so we can dance

and sing like children

tell stories

and be rejuvenated.

welcome to

the beginning of a new future

the universe

the infinite expanse

of the universe

beckons me

to discover

my place and

my purpose.

in the depth of my soul

i sense a quiet night.

at a distance

i hear the sounds of crickets.

i can feel

the chill of winter

and the warmth

of a bonfire.

my spirit is lifted

by the snowflakes

making their way

to the ground.

in that winter night

my soul beckons me

to surrender my ego

embrace my suffering

and reach out

to the universe

within and without.

in this journey

curiosity is my enabler

courage my companion

compassion my guide

and a heart filled with love

my savior.

i don't need to set goals

nor do i need

to measure progress

because no matter

how far i travel

there is no distance

between me and my destiny

i am free to wander

because

i am a part of the universe

and the universe

is a part of me

a poem within

a poem is an instinct

that's triggered within

when prose falls short

in conveying my feelings

it's less deliberate

and more spontaneous.

just like the moment

when i start singing and dancing

a poem nurtures the soul

by transforming

pain and suffering

restlessness and anger

into a sense of tranquility

just like the moment

when i sit by the ocean

feeling the vastness of the universe

sitting under the sky

and looking at the stars

makes me smile

my ego dissolves

and

a feeling of serenity

envelops me

a poem brings calmness

when the heart is ecstatic.

it brings humility

when we feel valiant

after we defeat an enemy

conquer lands

convert opponents

resolve a conflict

win people over

sway an audience or

tame an aggressor.

a poem is transcendental

it helps

notice without observing

understand without interpreting

express without analyzing

explain without rationalizing

a poem is an art

of touching from a distance

socrates believed

it was not wisdom

that enabled poets

to write their poetry

but a kind of instinct

or inspiration

such as you find

in seers and prophets

who deliver all their

sublime messages

without knowing in the least   *there is a poem in each of us*

what they mean   *waiting to be released*

an insight at haji ali

a seven year old me

holding my father's hand

made my first connection

with the ocean

while looking at the sunset

at the mosque of

haji ali

i remember

the tingling smell

the salty taste

and the shivering cold

as we stood there

watching the sun go down

when i looked up

i saw my father

pointing at the moon and he said:

whether it is a day or night

you can always find

a source of light

there will always be

a ray of hope

when everything

seems doomed

as the sun set

and the blurring line

of the horizon

faded into the darkness

i felt a sense of calm

i now know why.

my father's words

and the sound of the ocean

entrenched in my memory

a realization

that beyond every horizon

is a world to be discovered

and after every sunset

is a daybreak

waiting to inspire

and welcome me to

a new future

a new curiosity

a new intrigue and

a new discovery

i am still a child

i can wander without fear because

even when i'm lost

i remain curious

to explore my paths

expand my horizon

and find my way

i can start

without knowing

where i'm going because

i know there is more to see

than what i know exists

from that day

the sound of the ocean

resonates with me

just like the sound of om.

it awakens in me a curiosity

for the unknown

inner child

i can search and scan

my surroundings

without knowing

what i'm searching for because

i know there is more

to know and discover

than what i know

there is to find

i can fly without wings and

run with tired legs because

my imagination is free from

doubt fear or judgment

i'm never alone.

every human i've met

every moment i've lived

every story i've heard

and every memory i preserved

give me the energy

and the will

to be alive

to observe

to absorb

to share and

to spread

love and hope.

my nest egg is

my relationships

my memories and

my curiosity

i do not fear death

nor do i want to

prolong my life

because i know

till the last breath i'll retain   *and when it's time to go*

an irrepressible   *i will rest easy.*

enthusiasm for life   *i will sleep like a child*

pandemic

it's time to go back

to the basics

to be polite and

maintain distance

say namaste and

speak softly

so we contain

our own energy.

it's time to be mindful

of the consequences

of our own actions.

we may be young

strong and healthy

with thriving immunity

but we must know

what we bring home

for even though we may

suffer in social isolation

we may risk the lives

of our dearly beloveds.

we will be safer

in an air of altruism

it's time to be austere

to consume less

and conserve more

share our time and labor

for even though in shortage

of paper dollars

energy and time will thrive

that we will have more to learn. in this

we expand our imagination

we have more energy

to tinker with ideas

for a better future

suffer together

endure together

and one day

we rise together

it's time to reflect

reboot and reinvent.

take what's left

to invest in the new future

soul food

it's hard to look at

the positive side

when one is consumed with

negative emotions.

it's hard to feel optimistic

when one is overwhelmed with failure

or defeat.

it's hard to look for

a streak of light

when one is surrounded by darkness.

yet there is something

that helps the human heart.

a capacity we all have

that builds resilience and hope

strength and confidence.

expressing gratitude

nourishes the soul

redirects attention to

small acts which provide some

benefit feeling or convenience

just like little drops of water

make a mighty ocean

little words of gratitude

fill the heart with

a deep and vast contentment

welcome home

it's time

to rise above our egos

and think of ourselves

as a part of the ecosystem

to rise above our individuality

and think of ourselves

as part of the biosphere

it's time

to rise above seeing viruses as diseases

and think of them

as incompatible guests

who we invited to our bodies

by encroaching

upon their natural habitat

we won't

be able to rid our guests

nor avoid future visits

if we keep encroaching

on their habitat

if we keep destroying

their homes

where else will they go

but move into our bodies?

we must therefore

live and let live

a life of respectful

co existence.

let not our greed for conquering

for consuming

turn our bodies into their homes.

let us not

become the habitat

for something infectious

that wishes

only they will survive

and the human race

will be reduced to corpses

in the junkyard of history.

it's time to

rethink

reboot

and restrain our greed

one more chance

i asked a friend

how he was feeling

working remotely

from home.

he said:

it's interesting!

i'm getting used to it.

then he paused

for a moment and said

to be honest i'm going crazy

i thought to myself

i am not surprised.

we are trapped

with only the voices

in our heads.

they keep asking

difficult questions:

when will this end?

when it's all over

will it be

what it used to be?

do you want to

go back to

what it used to be?

and why?

what haunts us today is

not if we will die but

how we want to live

when it's all over

it's hard to face facts

our bodies are broken

our minds are exhausted

our souls are malnourished

it is obvious that

when it's all over

it won't be the same.

will i have a secure place

in the new future?

yes only if

i speak honestly

with my inner dialogue

with my dear ones

and with others

who are going crazy

facing their own

inner voices.

we have one more chance

to live purposefully before we die

a humanitarian crisis

they are

our neighbors yet

we treat them

as encroachers

as a blot

on the beauty

in our city

they cleaned

our homes

cooked for us

built our houses

manufactured the products

we use every day

constructed the roads

and the dams and the bridges.

they built the life we enjoy.

served us food

cleaned our streets

moved containers

that brought us goodies

from around the world

we complained

because they were

crowding our cities.

we mocked them

because they practice

a different culture.

we forced them

to speak our language

while we ridiculed theirs.

we want them to

adapt and assimilate.

they left their homes

and their land

so they could live a life

of dignity

and support their families

they lived in squalor

so their families

would not starve.

they lived with so little

so we could have

more than we need.

they suffered in poverty

while we enjoyed

upward mobility.

today we feel trapped

in our homes

because our jobs

and our ambitions

never gave us the time

to fully experience home

today we rush to stock up

toilet paper and hand sanitizers

because we have become

slaves to convenience

today as we practice

staying at home

handwashing and social distancing

they neither have homes

nor food.

they do not have water

nor do they have space

for social distancing.

from the comfort and luxury

of our homes

we log on the internet

and feel aghast at

millions of labor

crowding our streets

and buses and trains

to go back to their villages.

to go back to

the security of their families.

they believe

the villages they left behind

offer enough space to survive

and the cities they built

are at risk

of becoming

mass graves.

today they realize

that we are a risk

they can't live with.

today we realize

they are a lifeline

we can't live without

the real question

before us today is

while we obsess about

preserving our lives

and getting back to

our lifestyle

how might we protect

those who

we depend on

for our survival and pleasure?

while hiding in a bubble

a world apart

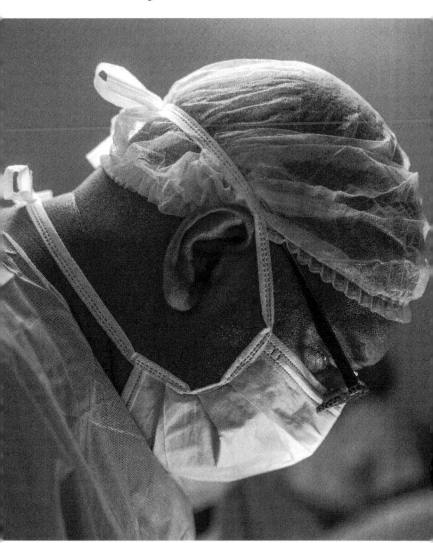

remembering those

who have spent our lives

pursuing happiness

searching for meaning

sailing beyond horizons

reaching out to the sky

expanding networks

growing assets

i can't stop thinking of those

who have spent their lives

building our dreams

serving our whims

carrying our egos

feeding our greed

sharing our burdens

nursing our wounds

we lament when

we don't get more

they despair when

they don't get enough

we lose hope

when we fear

losing what we have

they have no hope

even for what they need

to get by.

we feel vulnerable

stranded in our homes

they feel vulnerable because

they can't get home.

we wash our hands

ten times a day

while they stand

dripping with sweat

while we observe social distance

they run our supply chains

rush us in ambulances

police our streets

put out fires

drive food to us

sit at cash registers

terrified and vulnerable

we are worried

how long it will last

they are worried

how long they can last

i can't stop thinking of those

who live in a world

different from mine.

do we ever think

that to go upstairs

we push down on

the steps below?

without the steps

we could never

reach new heights.

it's high time

we think of those

we step upon

and leave behind

because without them

we would not be

where we want to be

the magic

we enter

an alternate state

of consciousness

when we take a break

from being awake

or from being real

or from being practical.

when we take a break

from our doubts

our fears

our pain

our beliefs

our prejudices

and social pressures

we gain freedom

to transcend

to an alternate universe.

our imagination

has no boundaries.

though it is not real

the feelings it creates

are real

the magic it creates

is real.

imagination is fueled by

curiosity and creativity.

our imagination

is not bound by time

it can be a mash up

of the past present and the future

of characters real and imaginary

of the things that seem

possible probable and impossible.

in our imagination

the fearful can become courageous

those in despair can gain hope

those who feel trapped

can find an escape

those in pain

can find relief

those who have a sinking feeling
can rise and fly.

for those who feel lost

a path may reveal itself

in their imagination.

shared imagination

inspires a shared purpose

a shared purpose

inspires collective action

collective action

creates momentum

to turn impossible into possible.

shared imagination

creates companionship and trust.

it unleashes a force for change

imagination

makes life worth living

makes hurdles worth crossing

makes pain worth bearing

makes mountains worth climbing.

imagination makes

cliffs worth diving off of

darkness worth diving into

and complexity and ambiguity

worth delving into

dare to imagine the future

no matter

how limited we feel

by mobility or energy

or finances

we all have one capacity

that will never hold us back

or drag us down:

the capacity to step out

of our reality and

into the world of imagination.

the capacity to imagine

the unimaginable

imagination can free us

from drudgery

from pain

from injustice.

from anger

from fear

from self doubt

from inaction

just one day

before his assassination

dr. king spoke —

i've been to the mountaintop...

and i've looked over.

and i've seen the promised land.

i may not get there with you.

but i want you to know tonight

that we as a people

will get to the promised land.

the power of imagination

brought him to this realization

even 27 years of

solitary confinement

could not keep mandela

from imagining

freedom from apartheid

to jonathan livingston seagull

imagination brought

a higher plane of existence

through perfection

of knowledge

imagination fuels

hope action and determination

imagination can help

resolve mysteries

dissolve disputes

explain complexities

unlock deadlocks

untangle mental blocks

explore alternatives and

inspire action.

the past

cannot be changed

though we can learn from it.

the present

will pass us quickly

the future holds

infinite possibilities

and abundant opportunities

for those who dare

to imagine it

in the midst of

pain and suffering

death and devastation

i see a sign

in the sighting of wildlife

in our cities

it occurred to me

that the fear of death

forced us to retreat

into our homes and

make space

for the wildlife

to discover

new freedom

it occurred to me

that we needed this retreat

so we can reflect on

what we've gained

and what we've lost

and create for us

a new purpose and

a new journey.

we now have

time to discover

the difference between

friends and friendships

wealth and richness

information and wisdom

connections and relations

goals and purpose

career and journey

success and growth

cooperation and collaboration

knowing and learning.

we can't be sure

what the future will be

but for sure the future is

open for reimagination.

the future will emerge

from a shared curiosity

that will evolve

through a dialogue

we can't predict the future

but we can be prepared for it

by starting a dialogue about

what we want to keep of the past

and what we want to leave behind

prepared for clarity

please recall a time when

you felt clarity

even for a moment

and ask why?

clarity to me

comes when

i am not blinded by

biases

prejudices

superstitions

emotions or

education

clarity to me

comes when

i am not deaf to

the voices around me

the rhythms of nature

the voice of my conscience

the notes that make a melody

clarity to me

comes when

i do not feel burdened by

my ego

my sorrow

my responsibilities

clarity to me

comes when

i am not constrained by

my past

my ideology

my comfort

i have experienced

moments of clarity when

my body is in a rhythm

(traveling in a train or dancing)

my mind is at a standstill

and i'm not seeking

answers to questions

solutions to problems or

a direction to the future.

i realize

that i cannot force clarity

i must tune my awareness

for clarity to appear

siddharth's truth

he gave up the glitter

in search of light.

even buddha's wisdom

could not illuminate his path.

he needed

his own journey

his own interpretation

and his own awakening

he walked a hundred miles and

climbed numerous mountains

after crossing rivers

siddhartha met vasudeva

all his life vasudeva ferried people

across the river.

he sat them in his boat

and talked to them about life

and set them off

on their quest

to vasudeva

river is timelessness.

to him the past the present

and the future are

only a moving shadow

of a steady soul

when siddhartha met vasudeva

he had walked far and wide

in search of truth

and of true love.

in vasudeva

he found a friend

who pointed him

to his path inward

to the truth within

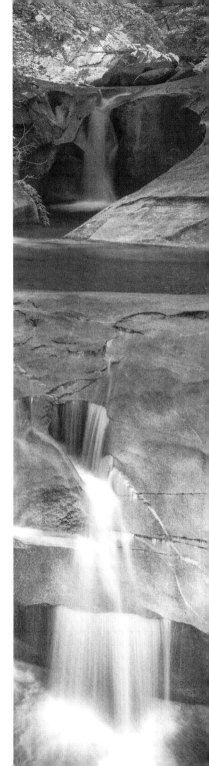

an awakened siddhartha

on his death bed

revealed to his friend govinda

that for every insight that

there is an opposite view

for every point

there is a counterpoint

for every idea

there is an alternative

for every belief

there is a doubt

that completes the truth

siddhartha found his truth

stillness

stillness

is nourishing

enlightening

illuminating and

has a presence

when the sun takes a dip

into the ocean at sunset

and snowflakes make their way down slowly

or leaves fall gently to the ground

and the stars twinkle mischievously

stillness

invites us to

discover our breath

activate compassion

forego thoughts

forget one's presence

and dissolve in atmosphere

in stillness we can discover

the magic of being

without being present

acknowledgments

i want to thank several people for their

contribution to this book. my wife rohini

persuaded me to compile my poems

into a book. our daughter isha and son in law

a. j., ash anderson and jeff borisch from

sonicrim provided feedback throughout. molly

pearson was an invaluable editorial

teammate in making this book what it is today.

through his visual design my friend

prof. mookesh patel brought alive the emotions

and intentions implicit in my poems.

i hope this book of poems serves as an

inspiration to appreciate the value of curiosity,

empathy, creativity and love.

uday dandavate

image credits

Printed in Poland
by Amazon Fulfillment
Poland Sp. z o.o., Wrocław